THE MILLIONAIRE Chick

For more information, or to book, contact :
Email: themillionairechickllc@gmail.com
Facebook: themillionairechick
Instagram: themillionairechick
YouTube: The Millionaire Chick

Donations or to support my ministry:
Cashapp: $realtorkimona
Paypal: kimonah

Book Design by TAB Intl Designs

Kimona Hanson

Table of Contents

Day of the week Prophetic Prayers:

"You Have Not Because You Asked Not." James 4:2

Thessalonians 5:19-21:
"Do not quench the Spirit. Do not treat prophecies with contempt but test them all; hold on to what is good."

Today the Holy Spirit shall Instruct you in the way to Go, and the Steps to take for your Breakthrough, Success, Testimony to Happen in Jesus name.

It doesn't matter what you have been through, I Declare your Season of Recovery, Breakthrough and Restoration in Jesus name.

Hey everyone,

I'm Kimona, and I'm excited to share with you the journey behind why I created this prophetic prayer journal. You see, for me, prayer has always been more than just words. It's been a lifeline, a channel through which I connect with God's heart and receive divine guidance. When I was younger, I learned a powerful way to deepen my prayer life with the ACTS method.

A - Adoration: Begin by praising God for who He is and His character. Express your love and awe for Him.
C - Confession: Acknowledge any sins or wrongdoings in your life and ask for forgiveness.
T - Thanksgiving: Thank God for His blessings in your life, both big and small.
S - Supplication: Finally, bring your requests and needs before God. Ask for His guidance and wisdom.

I created this journal because I've experienced firsthand the transformative power of prophetic prayers in my own life. In moments of uncertainty, confusion, and even despair, these prayers have been a beacon of hope, guiding me through the darkest of times and illuminating the path ahead.

But I didn't just want to keep this revelation to myself. I wrote this book with the intention of equipping you, my fellow journeyers, with the tools and insights needed to tap into the prophetic realm of prayer.

I believe that each of us has a unique God-given assignment, a purpose waiting to be fulfilled. And through the practice of prophetic prayers, we can align ourselves with God's will and walk confidently into our destinies.

So, what exactly are prophetic prayers, you ask? They're more than just petitions or requests; they're declarations of faith, inspired by the Holy Spirit, and spoken into existence with unwavering belief. Prophetic prayers have the power to shift atmospheres, break chains, and usher in God's kingdom here on earth.

In this journal, I'll guide you through the process of harnessing the power of prophetic prayers in your own life. From understanding the prophetic realm to practical tips on incorporating prophetic prayers into your daily routine, consider this your roadmap to a deeper, more intimate relationship with God and a more purposeful, fulfilling life.

So grab your journal, open your heart, and let's embark on this journey together. I can't wait to see how God will move in and through you as you unleash the power of prophetic prayers in your life.

Blessings,

Kimona

How to use this Prophetic Prayer Journal in 4 Steps:

1. Designate a specific time and place for prayer each day. Create a quiet and distraction-free environment where you can focus your attention on God.

2. Begin your prayer time by adoring God for who He is and His character. Reflect on His attributes such as love, mercy, and sovereignty. Use the Adoration section of the journal to guide your prayers and meditations.

3. Move on to confessing any sins or wrongdoings in your life and asking for forgiveness. Reflect on the areas where you may have fallen short and seek God's cleansing and renewal. Then, express gratitude to God for His blessings in your life, both big and small. Use the Confession and Thanksgiving sections of the journal to guide your prayers and reflections.

4. Finally, bring your requests and needs before God in supplication. Present your desires, concerns, and aspirations to Him, trusting in His provision and wisdom. Additionally, speak forth prophetic declarations of faith, aligning your prayers with God's promises and purposes for your life. Use the Supplication and Prophetic Declarations sections of the journal to guide your prayers and declarations.

By following these four steps and utilizing the prompts and guidance provided in the Prophetic Prayer Journal, you can deepen your prayer life, align with God's will, and experience the transformative power of prophetic prayers in your journey of faith.

Adoration

Adoration is the act of reverently worshiping and praising God for who He is. It involves recognizing His sovereignty, majesty, and attributes, and expressing awe and reverence towards Him. Adoration is an essential component of prayer, as it shifts our focus from ourselves to God and acknowledges His rightful place as the Creator and Sustainer of all things.

Scriptures:

- Psalm 95:6: Come, let us bow down in worship, let us kneel before the Lord our Maker.
- Psalm 96:9: Worship the Lord in the splendor of his holiness; tremble before him, all the earth.
- Revelation 4:11: You are worthy, our Lord and God, to receive glory and honor and power, for you created all things, and by your will they were created and have their being.

Meditations:

- Reflect on the attributes of God, such as His love, faithfulness, mercy, and sovereignty.
- Consider how God has revealed Himself in nature, through His Word, and in your personal experiences.
- Meditate on the greatness of God and His works, both in creation and in redemption.

Write out what comes to mind as you meditate on the scriptures.

 DATE:

_____

_____

_____

_____

_____

_____

_____

_____

_____

_____

_____

_____

Write out what comes to mind as you meditate on the scriptures.

 DATE:

_____

_____

_____

_____

_____

_____

_____

_____

_____

_____

_____

Write out what comes to mind as you meditate on the scriptures.

DATE:

_____

_____

_____

_____

_____

_____

_____

_____

_____

_____

_____

Prompts for Adoration in Prayer:

- Begin your prayer by declaring who God is and praising Him for His character and attributes.
- Express gratitude for specific ways God has demonstrated His love and faithfulness in your life.
- Invite the Holy Spirit to fill your heart with awe and reverence as you come into His presence.
- Use words of adoration from the Psalms or other passages of Scripture to guide your prayer.

Names of God & Characteristics of God:

- Wonderful God
- My Counselor
- Prince of Peace
- King of Glory Who Are You, You Are my Friend You Are my Sister
- Mighty God
- Lord of Lord
- Lillies of the valley
- Eternal rock of ages
- Lord of Host
- Rose Sharon
- Ancient of Days
- Bright Morning Star
- The Wisdom of God

Names of God & Characteristics of God Cont'd

- Our Healer
- Our Deliverer
- Our Provider
- Our Protector
- Our Defender
- Our Refuge
- Our Strength
- Our Creator
- Our Day Star
- Chief Corner Stone
- Righteous Judge
- Ageless God
- The Gracious God
- Merciful God
- Faithful God
- Our Consuming Fire
- Dependable God
- Reliable God
- Giver of Life
- Jehovah Ralph's
- Jehovah our Defender
- Our Instructor
- Adviser
- Director
- Lion of Judgeship
- Sustainer
- Restored
- Silencer
- Father to the fatherless

Names of God & Characteristics of God Cont'd

- Husband to the Wisdom
- The Way Truth and Light
- Bread of Life
- Winners of Winner
- Author and Finisher of our Salvation
- Glorious in Holiness Fearful in Praise
- Doing Wonders
- Sleepless God
- Ageless God
- Eternal God
- Excellent God
- Powerful God
- Compassionate God
- Worthy is our Lord
- Our Help Led
- He Is Richer than Rich
- He Is Stronger than the Strongest
- Higher than Highest
- Relentless God
- Master Builder
- Voice of God
- Alpha & Omega
- Game Changing God
- Our Fortress
- Strong Tower

Names of God & Characteristics of God Cont'd

- Unchanging God
- Pillar of Lives
- My Glory
- The Lifter of my Head
- The Bishop of my Soul
- Untimely God
- Ominpotent
- Omnipresent
- Ominiscent
- We Salute Your Excellency
- Always Doing Wonders
- He is Amen and Hallelujah
- Light in our Darkness
- Battle Stopper
- He is our Intercessions
- He Heals from our sin
- Jebohsbah ni

Example Adoration Prayer:

Lord God, I come before you with a heart full of adoration and awe. You are Jehovah-Jireh, the God who provides for all our needs. You are Jehovah-Rapha, the God who heals our brokenness and restores our souls.

You are El Shaddai, the Almighty God, whose power knows no bounds. You spoke the world into existence, and all things were created by you and for you. You are Yahweh, the great I AM, the Alpha and the Omega, the beginning and the end.

Thank you, Lord, for revealing yourself to us through your names. Each name reflects a different aspect of your character and nature. You are our Shepherd, our Healer, our Provider, and our Peace.

May our adoration and worship rise to you as a sweet fragrance. May our hearts overflow with gratitude for your goodness and mercy. In Jesus' name, amen.

Write out your adoration prayer while playing your favorite worship song.

DATE:

_____

_____

_____

_____

_____

_____

_____

_____

_____

_____

Write out your adoration prayer while playing your favorite worship song.

DATE:

_____

_____

_____

_____

_____

_____

_____

_____

_____

_____

Write out your adoration prayer while playing your favorite worship song.

_____

_____

_____

_____

_____

_____

_____

_____

_____

_____

Confession:

Confession is a vital aspect of the Christian faith, acknowledging the reality of sin and the need for repentance and forgiveness. It involves recognizing our wrongdoing, expressing remorse, and turning away from sin towards God. Confession opens the door to healing, restoration, and renewed fellowship with God.

Scriptures on Confession:

- Psalm 32:5: Then I acknowledged my sin to you and did not cover up my iniquity. I said, 'I will confess my transgressions to the Lord.' And you forgave the guilt of my sin.
- 1 John 1:9: If we confess our sins, he is faithful and just and will forgive us our sins and purify us from all unrighteousness.
- James 5:16: Therefore confess your sins to each other and pray for each other so that you may be healed. The prayer of a righteous person is powerful and effective.

Reflective Questions:

What areas of my life have I fallen short of God's standards?

_____

_____

_____

Are there patterns of behavior or attitudes that I need to confess and repent of?

_____

_____

_____

Reflective Questions:

How have my actions affected others, and how can I seek reconciliation?

_____

_____

_____

What barriers or obstacles hinder me from confessing my sins openly and honestly?

_____

_____

_____

Guidance on Confessing:

- Begin by acknowledging God's holiness and your need for His forgiveness.

- Reflect on specific sins or areas of disobedience in your life and confess them honestly to God.

- Express genuine remorse and a desire to turn away from sinful behaviors.

- Ask for God's forgiveness and grace to walk in obedience.

- Seek accountability and support from trusted individuals to help you grow in your journey of confession and repentance.

Example Confession Prayer:

Heavenly Father, I come before you with a contrite heart, acknowledging my need for your forgiveness and mercy. I confess that I have fallen short of your standards and have sinned against you in my thoughts, words, and actions.

Forgive me, Lord, for the times when I have neglected your commandments and pursued my own desires. I confess my pride, selfishness, and lack of love towards others. I repent of my sins and ask for your cleansing and renewal.

Help me, Lord, to walk in the light of your truth and to live a life that honors you. Give me the strength to resist temptation and the wisdom to make choices that align with your will. May my confession lead to transformation and restoration in my relationship with you and with others.

Thank you, Lord, for your abundant grace and forgiveness. May your love compel me to live a life of righteousness and obedience. In Jesus' name, amen.

Thanksgiving

Thanksgiving is more than just a holiday; it's a spiritual discipline that cultivates an attitude of gratitude in our hearts. When we approach God with thanksgiving, we acknowledge His goodness, faithfulness, and provision in our lives. Gratitude shifts our focus from what we lack to what we have, fostering contentment and joy.

Verses on Thanksgiving:

- Psalm 100:4: Enter his gates with thanksgiving and his courts with praise; give thanks to him and praise his name.
- 1 Thessalonians 5:18: Give thanks in all circumstances; for this is God's will for you in Christ Jesus.
- Psalm 107:1: Give thanks to the Lord, for he is good; his love endures forever.

Write Your Own Thanksgiving Prayer:

Here is my example:

Heavenly Father, I come before you with a heart overflowing with gratitude. You are the giver of every good and perfect gift, and I thank you for the countless blessings you have bestowed upon me.

Thank you, Lord, for the gift of life and breath, for each new day filled with opportunities to serve and glorify you. Thank you for the love of family and friends, for the relationships that bring joy and support into my life.

I am grateful, Lord, for your provision and sustenance, for the food on my table and the roof over my head. You have never failed to meet my needs, and I trust in your faithfulness to continue to provide for me.

Thank you, Father, for the gift of salvation through your Son, Jesus Christ. By his sacrifice on the cross, I am redeemed and forgiven, and I rejoice in the hope of eternal life with you.

Here is my example cont'd:

Lord, I thank you for the answered prayers and the moments of divine intervention in my life. You have been my rock and my refuge, my ever-present help in times of trouble.

May my life be a living testimony of your goodness and grace. Help me to cultivate a heart of gratitude in all circumstances, knowing that you are working all things together for my good.

I give you thanks and praise, now and forevermore. In Jesus' name, amen.

Write out your own thanksgiving prayer:

_____

_____

_____

_____

_____

_____

_____

_____

Write out your own thanksgiving prayer:

_____

_____

_____

_____

_____

_____

_____

Write out your own thanksgiving prayer:

_____

_____

_____

_____

_____

_____

_____

Supplication

Supplication is the act of earnestly and humbly making requests to God in prayer. It involves presenting our needs, desires, and concerns before the Lord, both for ourselves and for others. Supplication is a vital aspect of prayer, as it demonstrates our dependence on God and our trust in His provision and care.

Guidelines for Effective Supplication:

- Approach God with humility and sincerity, acknowledging your need for His help.
- Be specific in your requests, clearly articulating your needs and desires.
- Pray in faith, believing that God hears and answers prayers according to His will.
- Surrender your requests to God's sovereignty, trusting in His wisdom and timing.
- Intercede on behalf of others, lifting up their needs and concerns before the Lord.

Examples of Supplication Prayers:

- Prayers for physical healing for yourself or others who are sick or suffering.
- Requests for guidance and wisdom in decision-making and discerning God's will.
- Petitions for provision in areas of financial need, employment, or material provision.
- Intercession for family members, friends, and others who are facing challenges or difficulties.
- Appeals for spiritual growth, strength, and perseverance in the face of trials and temptations.

Prompts for Specific Requests:

- Reflect on areas of your life where you need God's intervention or assistance.
- Consider the needs of others around you, including family, friends, colleagues, and community members.
- Pray for the fulfillment of God's purposes and promises in your life and in the lives of others.
- Ask the Holy Spirit to guide your prayers and reveal areas of need that require supplication.

Example Supplication Prayer:

Heavenly Father, I come before you with a heart burdened with cares and concerns, knowing that you are the source of all help and hope. I lift up to you my personal needs and the needs of those around me, trusting in your unfailing love and provision.

Lord, I ask for healing and restoration in areas of my life where there is brokenness and pain. Grant me physical strength, emotional healing, and spiritual renewal, that I may walk in wholeness and freedom.

I pray for wisdom and discernment in the decisions I face, that I may align my will with yours and walk in obedience to your guidance. Lead me in the paths of righteousness, and open doors of opportunity according to your perfect plan.

Father, I bring before you the needs of my loved ones, [mention specific names or situations]. I ask for your protection, provision, and peace to surround them, and for your grace to sustain them in every trial and tribulation.

In all these things, Lord, may your name be glorified, and your kingdom come on earth as it is in heaven. Thank you for hearing my prayers and for your faithfulness to answer according to your perfect will. In Jesus' name, amen.

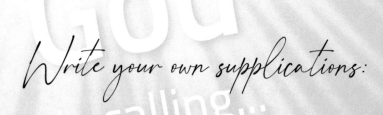

Write your own supplications:

Your Prayer Request to God...

_____

_____

_____

_____

_____

_____

_____

_____

Testimonies of Answered Prayers:

Share personal testimonies of answered prayers and blessings received.

_____

_____

_____

_____

_____

_____

_____

Testimonies of Answered Prayers:

Reflect on past experiences of answered prayers and how they have shaped your faith journey.

_____

_____

_____

_____

_____

_____

_____

_____

Urgent prophetic prayers are prayers offered with a sense of urgency and divine insight to address immediate and pressing needs. This section of the prayer journal equips believers to respond promptly to urgent situations with faith, boldness, and expectation of God's intervention.

Sample Urgent Prayers:

- Prayer for Healing: Lord, we lift up [name] who is in urgent need of healing. By your stripes, we declare their complete restoration and wholeness in Jesus' name.
- Prayer for Protection: Heavenly Father, surround [name or situation] with your hedge of protection. Guard them from harm and danger, and thwart every scheme of the enemy against them.
- Prayer for Provision: God, you are our provider, and we trust in your faithfulness to meet every need. Open doors of provision for [name or situation], and supply abundantly according to your riches in glory.

- Prayer for Peace: Prince of Peace, calm the storms that rage within and around [name or situation]. Let your peace that surpasses all understanding guard their hearts and minds in Christ Jesus.

Guidance on Discerning Urgent Needs:

- Pay attention to promptings of the Holy Spirit and feelings of urgency in your spirit.
- Seek confirmation through Scripture, prayer, and wise counsel before responding to urgent needs.
- Consider the potential impact and consequences of delayed action in addressing urgent situations.
- Trust in God's timing and sovereignty, knowing that He is always working for the good of those who love Him.

- Encouragement to Pray with Faith and Expectation
- Believe in the power of prayer to effect change and bring about God's purposes.
- Hold fast to God's promises and declarations of victory in Scripture.
- Pray with boldness and confidence, knowing that God hears and answers the prayers of His children.
- Anticipate breakthroughs, miracles, and divine interventions as you pray with faith and expectation.

Scriptures to Use:

- Philippians 4:6-7: Do not be anxious about anything, but in every situation, by prayer and petition, with thanksgiving, present your requests to God. And the peace of God, which transcends all understanding, will guard your hearts and your minds in Christ Jesus.

- Matthew 18:19-20: Again, truly I tell you that if two of you on earth agree about anything they ask for, it will be done for them by my Father in heaven. For where two or three gather in my name, there am I with them.
- James 5:16: Therefore confess your sins to each other and pray for each other so that you may be healed. The prayer of a righteous person is powerful and effective.

Sample Urgent Prayers:

Prayer for Protection:

Heavenly Father, we urgently lift up [name or situation] to you, asking for your divine protection and intervention. Surround them with your mighty angels, guarding them from all harm and danger. Foil every plan of the enemy and bring them safely through this trial. In Jesus' name, amen.

Prayer for Provision:

Lord God, we come to you in urgency, trusting in your promise to provide for all our needs. We lift up [name or situation], knowing that you are the source of every good gift. Open doors of provision and supply abundantly according to your riches in glory. Let your provision overflow in their lives for your glory. Amen.

Prayer for Healing:

Merciful God, we cry out to you in urgency for the healing of [name]. You are the Great Physician, and by your wounds, we are healed. Stretch forth your healing hand upon them, bringing restoration and wholeness to every part of their being. May your healing power be made manifest in their life for your glory. In Jesus' name, amen.

Prophetic Declarations:

Prophetic declarations involve speaking God's promises and truths into existence through faith-filled affirmations. These declarations are rooted in Scripture and are spoken with the expectation that God will bring them to fruition. By declaring God's Word over our lives and circumstances, we align ourselves with His will and invite His power to manifest in our lives.

Scriptural Declarations:

- Declare verses from Scripture that speak to specific promises or truths you are believing for.
- Choose passages that resonate with your situation and reflect God's faithfulness and power.
- Personalize the declarations by inserting your name or specific circumstances into the verses.

Affirmations of Faith

- Affirm your belief in God's goodness, faithfulness, and sovereignty.
- Declare your confidence in His ability to work all things together for your good.
- Speak words of victory, triumph, and breakthrough over challenging circumstances.

Guidance on Speaking Life into Challenging Circumstances:

- Speak from a place of faith, not fear, trusting in God's promises regardless of the circumstances.
- Be persistent in your declarations, even when facing obstacles or setbacks.
- Use the authority given to you as a believer to speak against negativity, doubt, and discouragement.
- Surround yourself with others who will support and affirm your declarations in prayer.

Example Prophetic Declarations:

Scriptural Declaration (Psalm 27:1):

The Lord is my light and my salvation; whom shall I fear? The Lord is the stronghold of my life; of whom shall I be afraid? I declare that God's light shines in the darkness of my circumstances, dispelling fear and bringing courage and confidence.

Example Prophetic Declarations:

Affirmation of Faith:

I declare that God is faithful to His promises. He is my provider, my healer, and my protector. I trust in His unfailing love and believe that He is working all things together for my good. I declare victory over every obstacle and breakthrough in every area of my life.

Prophetic Declaration (Isaiah 54:17):

No weapon formed against me shall prosper, and every tongue that rises against me in judgment I shall condemn. This is my heritage as a servant of the Lord, and my righteousness is from Him. I declare that every attack of the enemy is rendered powerless, and I walk in victory and authority as a child of God.

Destiny:

I declare that I am walking in alignment with God's perfect plan for my life. Every step I take is ordered by the Lord, and I am fulfilling my destiny and purpose. I am confident that God who began a good work in me will bring it to completion.

Children:

I declare that my children are blessed and highly favored by God. They are a heritage from the Lord, and I speak blessings, protection, and wisdom over their lives. They will grow up to be mighty in the land, fulfilling their God-given destinies.

Finances:

I declare that I am a steward of God's abundance, and His provision knows no bounds. I speak increase, prosperity, and abundance over my finances. Every financial need is met according to His riches in glory, and I am blessed to be a blessing.

Wealth:

I declare that I am walking in divine wealth and abundance. I am blessed to be a channel of God's prosperity, and I receive His favor and blessings in every area of my life. I am prospering spiritually, mentally, physically, and financially, in Jesus' name.

Real Estate:

I declare that God has given me the ability to acquire and manage real estate properties for His glory. I speak blessings and success over every real estate venture I undertake. Every property I own is a testimony of God's faithfulness and provision in my life.

DAY OF THE WEEK
Prophetic Prayers:

Weekly prayer focuses tailored to specific themes and needs, designed to guide believers in seeking God's guidance, provision, and intervention in various areas of life.

MONDAY

Commanding the Week Prophetic Prayers

↓

Prayer for Divine Direction:

Heavenly Father, as I begin this new week, I declare your sovereign authority over my life. Lead me and guide me in the paths of righteousness. Grant me clarity of vision to discern your will and wisdom to make decisions that honor you. Let your Holy Spirit direct my steps, and may I walk in obedience to your commands. In Jesus' name, amen.

DAY OF THE WEEK

Prophetic Prayers:

MONDAY

Commanding the Week Prophetic Prayers

Prayer for Authority and Favor:

Lord God, I declare that I am seated with Christ in heavenly places, far above all principalities and powers. I command every obstacle and hindrance to my success to be removed in Jesus' name. Grant me favor and breakthroughs in every area of my life this week. Let your kingdom come and your will be done in my life. Amen.

---- MONDAY ----

Commanding the Week Prophetic Prayers

Prayer for Productivity and Success:

Dear Lord, I commit this week into your hands, trusting in your provision and guidance. I declare that I am empowered by your Spirit to accomplish all that you have planned for me. Grant me productivity, efficiency, and success in my endeavors. Help me to glorify you in all that I do. In Jesus' name, amen.

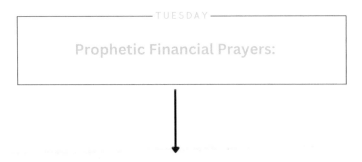

Prayer for Provision and Abundance:

Heavenly Father, I lift up my financial needs to you today, knowing that you are my provider. I declare your promises of provision and abundance over my life. Open doors of opportunity and pour out blessings beyond measure. Grant me wisdom to steward your resources wisely. Thank you for meeting all my needs according to your riches in glory. Amen.

DAY OF THE WEEK

Prophetic Prayers:

Prophetic Financial Prayers:

Prayer for Debt Freedom and Financial Freedom:

Lord, I declare freedom from debt and financial bondage in Jesus' name. I break every chain of debt and lack that has held me captive. Release supernatural provision and resources to pay off debts and live in financial abundance. Thank you for your faithfulness to supply all my needs according to your glorious riches. Amen.

DAY OF THE WEEK

Prayer for Generosity and Kingdom Impact:

Father, help me to be a cheerful giver and a faithful steward of the resources you have entrusted to me. I declare a spirit of generosity and abundance over my finances. Use me to bless others and advance your kingdom purposes on earth. May my giving bring glory to your name and bear eternal fruit. In Jesus' name, amen.

DAY OF THE WEEK

DAY OF THE WEEK

Prophetic Prayers:

Prophetic Prayers for Children:

Prayer for Protection and Safety:

Heavenly Father, I lift up my children [name them] to you today, asking for your divine protection and safety. Surround them with your angels and shield them from harm and danger. Guard their hearts and minds against negative influences, and lead them in the paths of righteousness. May they walk in your truth and grow in wisdom and stature before you and others. Amen.

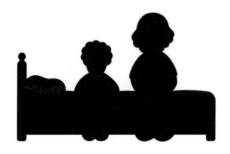

DAY OF THE WEEK

Prophetic Prayers:

WEDNESDAY

Prophetic Prayers for Children:

Prayer for Wisdom and Guidance:

Lord, I pray for wisdom and guidance for my children as they navigate through life's challenges and decisions. Grant them discernment to make wise choices and to seek your will in all things. Help them to hear your voice and to follow your leading. May they walk in obedience to your commands and fulfill the purpose and destiny you have for their lives. Amen.

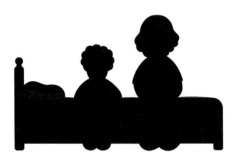

DAY OF THE WEEK
Prophetic Prayers:

Prophetic Prayers for Children:

Prayer for Spiritual Growth and Salvation:

Father, I lift up my children's spiritual growth and salvation to you, knowing that salvation is your heart's desire for all. I declare that they will come to know you personally and experience the life-transforming power of your love and grace. Draw them to yourself, Lord, and open their eyes to see the beauty of your salvation. May they walk in the light of your truth and serve you all the days of their lives.
Amen.

Prophetic Prayers for Marriage/Spouse:

Prayer for Unity and Harmony:

Lord, I lift up my marriage to you today, asking for your grace and wisdom to cultivate unity and harmony. I declare that love and understanding will abound between my spouse and me. Help us to communicate with kindness and patience, and to forgive one another as you have forgiven us. Strengthen the bond of love between us, Lord, and let your peace reign in our home. Amen.

Prayer for Strength and Endurance:

Father, I pray for strength and endurance for my marriage in the face of challenges and trials. Grant us the grace to persevere through difficult times and to lean on you for support and guidance. Fill us with your love and compassion for one another, and help us to bear each other's burdens. May our marriage be a testimony of your faithfulness and grace. Amen.

DAY OF THE WEEK
Prophetic Prayers:

Prophetic Prayers for Marriage/Spouse:

Prayer for Restoration and Healing:

Heavenly Father, I bring before you any areas of brokenness or strife in my marriage. I declare healing and restoration over every wounded heart and fractured relationship. Pour out your grace and mercy, Lord, and mend what is broken. Help us to forgive one another and to rebuild trust and intimacy. May our marriage be a reflection of your love and redemption. Amen.

———————

These weekly prophetic prayers provide a structured framework for believers to engage with God in seeking His intervention and blessings in various aspects of life. Through consistent prayer and faith-filled declarations, believers can align themselves with God's will and experience His power and provision in their lives and communities.

Prophetic Prayers for the Nation

Prayer for Government Leaders:

Heavenly Father, we lift up our government leaders to you today, asking for wisdom, discernment, and integrity to guide their decisions and actions. Grant them a heart for justice, righteousness, and compassion towards all people. May they govern with humility and seek the common good of our nation. Strengthen and empower them to lead with wisdom and courage. Amen.

Prayer for Peace and Unity:

Lord, we pray for peace and unity to prevail in our nation, despite differences in opinions, beliefs, and backgrounds. Break down barriers of division and hostility, and bring reconciliation and healing to our land. Let your love and grace transform hearts and minds, leading to understanding and cooperation among all people. May our nation be a beacon of harmony and unity in a divided world. Amen.

DAY OF THE WEEK

Prophetic prayers:

Prophetic Prayers for the Nation

Prayer for Revival and Spiritual Awakening:

Father, we cry out for revival and spiritual awakening in our nation. Pour out your Spirit upon us, igniting a passion for righteousness and holiness. Stir hearts to seek you earnestly and turn from wickedness. Let your light shine brightly in every corner of our nation, drawing people to yourself and transforming lives. May our nation experience a great spiritual awakening that leads to lasting revival and renewal. Amen.

DAY OF THE WEEK

Prophetic Prayers:

Prophetic Prayers for Homeownership

Here are five prophetic prayers for a homeownership.

Prayer 1:

Dear God, I pray that my new home and land would be a place of abundance and prosperity, just as Psalm 112:3 says, Wealth and riches are in their house, and their righteousness endures forever. Let my home be a place where your blessings overflow, and where I can share your love and provision with others. In Jesus' name, I pray. Amen.

Prayer 2:

Father God, I declare that my new home and land are debt-free, just as Romans 13:8 says, Let no debt remain outstanding, except the continuing debt to love one another. Let my financial affairs be in order, and may I be a good steward of the resources you have given me. In Jesus' name, I pray. Amen.

Prophetic Prayers for Homeownership

Prayer 3:
Lord, I pray that my new home and land would be a place of generational wealth and blessing, just as Proverbs 13:22 says, A good person leaves an inheritance for their children's children. Let my home be a place where your love and provision are passed down to future generations, and where your blessings never end. In Jesus' name, I pray. Amen.

Prayer 4:
Dear Heavenly Father, I pray that my new home and land would be a place of prosperity and success, just as Joshua 1:8 says, Keep this Book of the Law always on your lips; meditate on it day and night, so that you may be careful to do everything written in it. Then you will be prosperous and successful. Let my home be a place where your Word is honored, and where your love and grace are always present. In Jesus' name, I pray. Amen.

Prophetic Prayers for Homeownership

Prayer 5:
God, I declare that my new home and land are blessed and favored by you, just as Psalm 84:11 says, For the Lord God is a sun and shield; he bestows favor and honor. No good thing does he withhold from those who walk uprightly. Let my dwelling place be a place of joy and celebration, where your presence is always felt and your love is always shared. In Jesus' name, I pray. Amen.

Remember, prayer is a powerful tool, and God is always with you, guiding and directing you. May these prayers bring you comfort, peace, and blessings as you embark on this new journey to your new home and land.

Prophetic Prayers for Homeownership

Here are the 10 powerful prophetic declarations for homeownership.

1. I declare this home is a place of blessings, where God's favor and love will always abide.

2. I declare our family is debt-free, and we will manage our finances wisely, always trusting in God's provision.

3. I declare this home is a hub of generational wealth, and we will use our resources to bless others and further God's kingdom.

4. I declare this home is dedicated to God, and we invite His presence and guidance in all aspects of our lives.

5. I declare abundance and prosperity in this home, and we will always have more than enough to meet our needs and share with others.

6. I declare our family and all who enter this home blessed, favored, and protected by God's love and grace.

7. I declare this home is a place of wisdom, knowledge, and understanding, and we will seek God's guidance in all our decisions.

Prophetic Prayers For Homeownership

Here are the 10 powerful prophetic declarations for homeownership.

8. I declare freedom from debt and financial stress in this home, and we will live with peace and joy.

9. I declare unity and love in this home, where our family will be strengthened and our relationships will flourish.

10. I declare this home is a place of legacy, where we will build a heritage of faith, love, and prosperity for generations to come.

Remember, speaking these declarations out loud with faith and conviction will help to bring God's blessings and favor into your new home!

How to Command Your Day & Week

You should never have a bad day in your life in the name of Jesus. To take charge of your day, you must be an early riser. Those who rise early to seek God witness His power and glory throughout the day. In Job 38:12, it says "Have you commanded the morning since your days began, and caused the dawn to know its place?" Command your morning and prepare for success daily.

Preparation is key to success; you must prepare spiritually. You must invoke spiritual laws to override any satanic laws opposing your life and destiny. Life is spiritual, with forces fighting us daily.God has given you the authority to command your day and direct its course. This is why it's essential to command your day, and to never leave your house casually. This spiritual discipline fortifies you, changing your story. Never leave your home without commanding your day or week. Make this your lifestyle, and your life will transform.

Let's Begin to Command Your Day

Start by thanking God.
God I'm thankful for today.
We bless your holy name.
Take all the glory and honor.
Thank you father.
Thank you Jesus.
Thank him for your life and for waking you up.
Start to speak into your day.
Give direction to your day.
Mention the day and say I take authority of the day.
Take authority over this day.
Say today will be a good day.
I draw upon heavenly resources.
I shall not lack today.
I will win today.
Favor will locate me today.
New opportunities will attract me today.

Let's Begin to Command Your Day

My business with flourish.
I shall meet good people today.
Whatever I'm pursuing today I should get it.
Angel move four corners to bring me customers.
Open my eyes to see the strategies.
I will break through in my business.
I will breakthrough in my career.
I'm heavenly protected and angels are watching over me &
my family.
Everything that has a name must listen.
Monday hear me you should favor me.
Tuesday you should give me what I desire.
Wednesday this day should produce the results I'm
expecting.
Thursday this day should be a good day for blessings.
Friday this day should financially favor me.
Saturday this day should be a supernatural day for me.
Sunday this day should be a successful day for me.
I speak blessings into my day.

Visualization Exercise: Commanding Your Week

Find a Quiet Space: Choose a quiet and comfortable space to meditate on scripture that **supports your declarations for** the week. Write them here.

_____

_____

_____

_____

_____

_____

_____

Visualization Exercise: Commanding Your Week

Prepare Your Heart: Take a few moments to center yourself and prepare your heart for prayer. Close your eyes and take several deep breaths to calm your mind and spirit. Write them down here.

_____

_____

_____

_____

_____

_____

_____

Visualization Exercise: Commanding Your Week

Set Intentions: Begin by setting your intentions for the upcoming week. **What do you hope to accomplish?** What challenges do you anticipate? Invite God into this process and ask for His guidance and wisdom. Write down what you envisioned.

_____

_____

_____

_____

_____

_____

_____

_____

Visualization Exercise: Commanding Your Week

Visualize Success: Visualize yourself stepping into the new week with confidence and authority. See yourself overcoming obstacles, achieving your goals, and walking in alignment with God's will. Imagine each day filled with divine appointments, opportunities for growth, and moments of joy and blessing. Write them down here.

_____

_____

_____

_____

_____

_____

_____

Visualization Exercise: Commanding Your Week

Declare God's Promises: Speak aloud **declarations of faith and victory** over the week ahead. Declare God's promises of provision, protection, and favor over every aspect of your life. Command blessings to manifest, obstacles to be removed, and divine opportunities to arise. Write down what your releasing.

_____

_____

_____

_____

_____

_____

_____

Visualization Exercise: Commanding Your Week

Release Control: Surrender control of the week to God, trusting in His sovereignty and faithfulness. Let go of any anxiety or worry, knowing that He is in control and will work all things together for your good. Write down what your grateful for.

_____

_____

_____

_____

_____

_____

_____

Express Gratitude: Conclude the exercise by expressing gratitude to God for His presence, provision, and promises. Thank Him for the opportunity to partner with Him in commanding the week ahead.

_____

_____

_____

_____

_____

_____

_____

Make this visualization exercise a weekly practice as you engage in Commanding the Week Prophetic Prayers. It can serve as a powerful tool for setting intentions, aligning with God's will, and stepping into the week with confidence and authority.

Kimona

Reflection and Gratitude Exercise: Celebrating Your Journey

Set Aside Time: Find a quiet and comfortable space where you can reflect without distractions. Set aside dedicated time for this activity.

Take a moment to flip through the pages of your prophetic prayer journal and reflect on the journey you've embarked on. Recall the prayers you've prayed, the prophetic declarations you've spoken, and the ways God has moved in your life.

Celebrate the victories, answered prayers, and breakthroughs you've experienced along the way. Take note of how God has been faithful to His promises and has shown Himself strong on your behalf.

Acknowledge the ways in which you've grown spiritually and emotionally throughout this journey. Reflect on the lessons learned, the challenges overcome, and the insights gained.

Take time to express gratitude to God for His faithfulness, provision, and presence throughout your journey. Thank Him for every answered prayer, every moment of guidance, and every instance of His grace.

Write a heartfelt letter to God, expressing your gratitude, love, and devotion. Pour out your heart to Him, thanking Him for His goodness and faithfulness. Share your hopes, dreams, and aspirations for the future.

Conclude the activity by offering a prayer of dedication and commitment to God. Surrender your life, your dreams, and your future into His hands, trusting in His perfect plan and timing.

Write a letter to God. . .

Bonus: Wealth Affirmation

The Bible says Psalms 112:3, "Wealth and riches will be in his house, And his righteousness endures forever."

You are a powerfully intelligent people that can moves mountains!

When you speak... creations begins again.

How do I know this? Because we were all born with the energy to speak things into existence and call things into being. Job 22:28 says, "You will also declare a thing, And it will be established for you."

I now have ten powerful wealth affirmations that have transformed my life, elevating me from a state of lack to experiencing six-figure months in my business.

Here they are:

1. I cannot help but attract a lot of money into my life!
2. I always have more money than I need because God is my provider!
3. I cannot help, but to attract a lot money into my life because I am a lender and not a borrower!
4. I am a money magnet and money is always attracted to me all the time!
5. Money is my birthright and God is my supplier!
6. My income is constantly increasing!
7. I am prosperous in every area of my life!
8. Everyday I am becoming wealthier!
9. Money comes to me easily and effortlessly!
10. I am a Millionaire!

Repeat these affirmations three times daily for the next seven days, and then share your testimony with me via email. You will witness remarkable results through the power of faith and affirmation.